**Creating in Collage**

# Creating in Collage

Natalie d'Arbeloff

with illustrations by Jack Yates

Studio Vista London

Watson–Guptill Publications New York

General Editor Jean Richardson
© Natalie d´Arbeloff and Jack Yates 1967
Published in London by Studio Vista Limited
Blue Star House, Highgate Hill, London N19
and in New York by Watson-Guptill Publications
165 West 46th Street, New York 10036
Distributed in Canada by General Publishing Co. Ltd
30 Lesmill Road, Don Mills, Toronto, Ontario
Library of Congress Catalog Card Number 68-10159
Set in Univers 8 and 9 pt.
by V. Siviter Smith & Co. Ltd, Birmingham
Printed in the Netherlands
by N. V. Grafische Industrie Haarlem

# Contents

# Introduction

The name 'collage' is derived from the French word for glue, 'colle'. Making a collage is a process of selecting, assembling, and pasting down pieces of paper or almost any other material.

The result may be a work of art, a decoration, a means of communication, or simply a game. Given a variety of odds and ends, a few magazines, a pair of scissors and a pot of glue, anyone can put together a pleasing, amusing or startling arrangement. The magical ease of the technique prejudices some people against collage as a serious art form; they declare that profound works can never be produced in a medium so dependent on the accidental. But the accidental element is present only if the collagist allows it to be. You can, if you wish, make collages that are planned and controlled from start to finish. Or, you can 'play by ear' and just see what happens. No other creative technique is so versatile and so responsive to every temperament.

The only way to find out what you can do with collage, and to know whether it will turn out to be your hobby or your principal interest, is by experimenting and by looking at the results others have achieved. This book aims to help you to do just that, by suggesting a variety of experiments applying the various techniques of collage, and by including as many examples as possible of work by contemporary artists, by students, and by some of the pioneers, or 'old masters', in this field.

# 1 Collecting materials

The finding and selecting of materials for collage is a fascinating process in itself. You could begin collecting bits and pieces of anything at all, or be guided by specific ideas you want to carry out. Either way, your choice of materials is as individual as the manner in which you use them; the process of making a collage begins the moment you start looking around for likely materials. Here is a general list of some of them.

### Paper

All the scraps you can find in your desk-drawers, or rescue from the wastepaper basket (e.g., bills, grocery lists, letters, stamped envelopes, greeting cards, snapshots, labels). These fragments and cast-offs from your daily life hold all sorts of associations which you can use to create wonderful visual 'poems'. The master of collage-poetry was Schwitters (see p. 88), who transformed the most commonplace materials and showed that nothing is despicable.

A pile of newspapers and magazines provides another instantly available source of collage material. Unwanted books, prints, drawings and photographs might be very useful; ask your friends to let you have their throw-outs. If photography is your hobby, you will find that discarded negatives, film-packets, photographic papers, etc., have possibilities as collage elements.

Other materials which you most likely have on hand or can easily obtain are tissue-paper, aluminium foil, sandpaper, corrugated cardboard, wallpaper samples.

Finally, there are all the 'art papers' sold in art and craft supply shops. Whether or not you will need a stock of these depends on your own preferences and on the results of your experiments. For a start, you could buy only one or two sheets of any type of paper whose colour or texture appeals to you; for example, tinted pastel paper, poster paper, vellum or parchment, Japanese paper, etc. (Most well-equipped art supply stores have paper sample books which you can choose from.) A packet of construction paper in assorted colours is always useful.

Fig. 1 Jack Yates: *Souvenirs.*

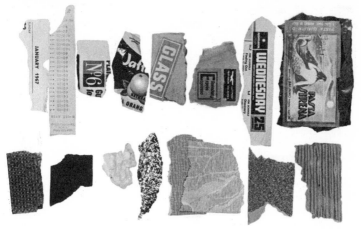

Fig. 2 Samples of found paper.

Fig. 3 Student, Camden Arts Centre: *Warrior*. Scraps of wood from packing crates.

## Natural forms

Driftwood, tree bark, leaves and seed pods, dried grasses, shells, feathers, chips of stone and coloured glass, scraps of metal, and so on, offer an endless variety of shapes, colours and textures and suggest moods which can be the start of a collage. At times, the addition of even a single 'natural form' will make a collage

10

suddenly seem just right. If you live in a large city, you may have to go to a bit of trouble to find these natural materials, but an exploration of building sites and public parks can be rewarding. A local carpenter or wood-yard will often let you have the odd bits and pieces, of no use to anyone but yourself.

## Fabrics

Remnants of every kind can be incorporated in collages. Chapter 5 will describe some of the possibilities of fabrics. Save all your old dress or upholstery scraps, and pieces of net stockings, lace, string vests, printed cottons, towelling, leather, PVC, oilcloth and hessian (burlap). Filmy, transparent materials, such as nylon, create beautiful contrasts of tone when laid over solid colours; rayons and satins, gold and silver lamés, reflect the light and make opulent, sensuous surfaces. Printed fabrics ought to be used with discretion, as the profusion of their patterns and ready-made designs tend to weaken the role of the imagination.

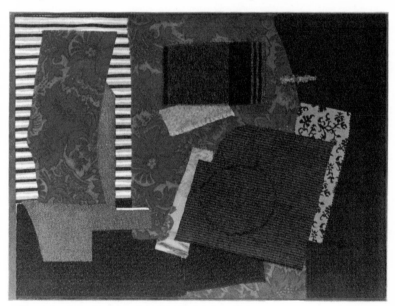

Fig. 4 Student, Camden Arts Centre: fabric collage.

## Found objects

This heading covers such a vast variety that a complete list (if such a thing were possible) would read somewhat like a 'Sears-Roebuck' catalogue in several volumes. For purposes of attaching to a flat surface, anything that is small and reasonably lightweight can be used. Larger and heavier objects, which are not necessarily fixed to a background but can be grouped together in 'assemblages', are dealt with in chapter 7. Your collection of 'found' objects could include items like these: bottle caps, buttons, spools, pipe-cleaners, nuts and bolts, costume jewelry, badges, buckles, small gift boxes, playing cards, toys, letters and numbers. Besides all the things you can find in your own household, there is also the dazzling array of inexpensive trinkets which you can purchase from the 'notions' counters of any department store or Woolworths.

Fig. 5 Natalie d'Arbeloff: *Cut this out*. Paper and found objects.

## Storing materials

This can present a problem, especially if space is limited and the 'collecting mania' very strong. The solution is to devise some kind of system in accordance with your own personality and method of working. This will avoid confusion and frustrating searches for one particular scrap which you know you have, but can't remember where you've put it.

You could, for example, classify your materials according to the general headings given in this chapter, i.e., paper, natural forms, fabrics, and found objects. (A roomy chest of drawers makes a good storage cabinet.) Rather than accumulate an enormous pile of magazines and newspapers, you could go through your stock and tear out only those pages or pictures which you think you will need, then file these away under titles such as 'eyes', 'trees', 'buildings'. Some items might be grouped together for colour, texture or shape. For example, the colour 'red' could include red fabrics, red bottle-tops, reddish wood, illustrations in which red predominates. Do not think that you are wasting time or being needlessly methodical in devising these systems; you have, perhaps, visited artists whose studios are full of disorganized clutter, which does not seem to impede their creative activity in any way. This may be so in the case of artists who know very clearly what they are aiming at, but if you are just beginning to explore the process of creation, any system which can stimulate and develop your interest in form, colour, and composition is helpful.

Making a personal inventory of your collage materials, with a view to what roles they might eventually play, is a worthwhile and fascinating project, which can lead you to the invention of many more experiments than the ones described in this book.

Fig. 6 Collage screen.

# 2 Equipment

The only rule concerning equipment for making collages is that you ought to have a rigid support and a good quality adhesive. But even this rule is elastic, and many excellent collages are produced using the cheapest paste on whatever scrap of paper happens to be on hand. So if you feel inspired to begin at once, by all means do so, using any sheet of cardboard or paper for your support, and any kind of paste. As you progress with your experiments, you will discover what type of equipment is most suitable to your particular needs. The list given below can serve as a general guide.

## 1 Supports

Hardboard (Masonite), plywood, chipboard, Perspex (Plexiglas), glass, linoleum, stretched canvas, or any other flat, non-warping surface. Heavy paper and cardboard ought to be mounted to a rigid backing. Wall-surfaces, tiles, table-tops, doors, screens, cupboards, lampshades, boxes, etc. can be decorated with collage.

## 2 Adhesives

For try-outs and any temporary pasting down, a rubber solution (such as Cow Gum) is essential, as it may be removed when dry by rubbing with the fingers.

For general purposes, there are many excellent, quick-drying, glues on the market (Casco, Copydex, Sobo). For thick or heavy materials, use a contact adhesive (both surfaces must be coated with the glue), but remember that you cannot move the pieces once they have been pressed together. The contact adhesives (Evo-Stik, UHU glue, Weldwood) are very strong and will bond together different types of materials.

## 3 Paints and varnishes

Any type of paint may be used in combination with collage. Most useful of all are the acrylic-polymer colours (Rowney Cryla Colours or Liquitex). These are permanent, quick-drying, and can be used on practically any surface (paper, cloth, board, canvas, etc.). They are mixed with water, require no special solvents, and most important to the collagist, have tremendous powers of adhesion which increase with age; bits of paper, etc., may be stuck directly into the wet colours.

All collages ought to be given some final protective coating. Here again, the acrylic-polymer mediums and varnishes are excellent. They strengthen and waterproof paper surfaces, imparting a gloss or matt finish to the work (several types are available, such as Cryla No. 1 Gloss Medium, or No. 2 Matt Medium, etc.). Any art-supply shop will give you leaflets about acrylic products, which are now manufactured by most of the leading artists' materials firms. When applied, this type of varnish appears as a milky liquid, but it dries in a matter of minutes to a clear, transparent film.

## 4 Tools

Only the simplest tools are required for collage:

A good sharp pair of scissors with a blade of not less than 4"

An all-purpose knife or a stencil cutting knife such as the one illustrated

A wooden or rubber roller is not essential, but useful for flattening pasted surfaces

A sponge (rags will do as well)

A cupcake baking-tin makes a handy palette for diluting glues, colours, etc. You will also need a few containers of any sort.

A few brushes: a paste brush; a household brush (approx. 3") for varnishing large areas; one or two flat bristle brushes

A palette knife

Pencils, pens, crayons, or whatever drawing materials you wish to use.

You can achieve excellent results with a minimum of equipment and expense.

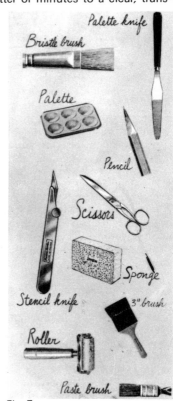

Fig. 7

15

# 3 Cut-paper collage

The cut-paper technique produces clean, definite, 'hard-edged' contours, and is most suited to making collages where the emphasis is on bold design and strong contrasts of colour. The simple experiment given below could be a starting point in your exploration of the possibilities of this method.

**Experiment 1**

1  You will need a rigid support for your collage: any good paper adhesive and several sheets of fairly stiff coloured paper (construction paper will do).
2  Cut your coloured paper into a few, simple, related shapes (fig. 8). The still-life illustrated is only an example, you can change or adapt this subject to suit yourself. Use your scissors boldly, 'drawing' with them as you go. You can, if you prefer, make a preliminary sketch, but you will benefit more from this exercise if you use the scissors as your only drawing tool.
3  Arrange your cut-outs on the support (figs. 9, 10). You may find you have too many shapes, or not enough; make new ones, or take some away. Put some shapes over others, try different combinations of colour, add a detail here and there. Do not be in too great a hurry to make a 'finished picture': the value of these experiments is in what you discover during the process of carrying them out. If you are pleased with the result, it will not be because you have followed instructions, but because you have put a great deal of yourself into the work.
4  When you are satisfied with your composition as a whole, paste all the pieces down on the support (fig. 11), and allow to dry. Finally, pour a little varnish (see p. 15) into a saucer, put the picture flat and lay on the varnish with a flat, semi-stiff, one inch brush.

You could try similar experiments with different types of paper: wrapping paper, magazine pages, newsprint, etc., searching for variety in colour and pattern. Practise 'drawing' with scissors until it seems as natural to you as holding a pencil.

Coloured tissue-paper has many possibilities. You can use it on its own (as in fig. 13), allowing some edges to overlap, creating subtle colour variations. Or, you can combine it with coloured and printed papers for a misty, clouded effect. You can

Fig. 8

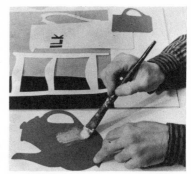

Fig. 11

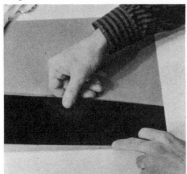

Fig. 9

Fig. 12 Finished work.

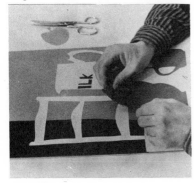

Fig. 10

crumple and wrinkle its surface after you have pasted it down (pushing it with your fingers or the handle of a brush) to produce relief textures. Use paste or Cow Gum (rubber cement) for tissue-paper, in very thin applications.

Symmetrical shapes, such as the bottles in the illustration below, are arrived at by folding the paper in half and cutting out half of the shape; when the paper is unfolded, the two halves match exactly. Try making stylized figures and objects in this manner; you will be surprised at the enormous variations possible. This is the same principle as the 'paper dolls' which children cut out; you can derive the same enjoyment from it, and at the same time develop your sense of design.

The fact that simple paper cut-outs can become a wonderfully expressive visual language was proved beyond a doubt by Matisse (see p. 94), whose masterful 'papiers collés' (pasted papers) are a monument to this form of collage.

Fig. 13 Jack Yates: *Bottles*. Coloured tissue paper.

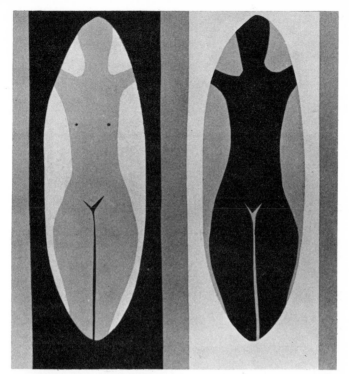

Fig. 14 Jack Yates: *Oval motif.* Coloured paper.

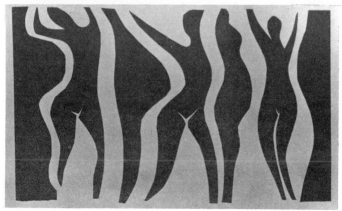

Fig. 15 Jack Yates: *Dancers.* Coloured paper.

## Experiment 2

Working from life with cut paper is a fascinating process, even for those who think they 'can't draw a straight line'. The fact that you are limited to scissors, paper and paste obliges you to interpret the shapes you see around you in a simplified way, and to 'construct' your picture out of them, much as you might use building blocks. You will find yourself spontaneously inventing symbols that represent a particular shape without describing its every detail. In this process, you will understand from first-hand experience what many of the modern art movements are about (not only modern, but art of *all* times has been concerned with problems of interpretation and simplification).

For this exercise, have on hand several sheets of paper that contrast with each other in tone (e.g., newspaper, brown wrapping paper, white tissue, plain white paper, black paper). A good subject to start with would be the room in which you are sitting; decide which angle interests you most, and install yourself comfortably before it. Once again, I would suggest that you do not make a preliminary sketch, but start cutting directly. Use the different tones of paper to indicate the lights and darks of your subject. Cut out some big, simple shapes to represent the background (walls, carpet, windows, etc.) Where you want grays or patterns, use the newspaper, which can liven up your composition in surprising ways.

You can glue the paper shapes down as you go (largest areas first), or wait until you have done all the cutting out you want to do and then put them in place. Look at your work from a distance occasionally (a few dabs of Cow Gum will keep the pieces down temporarily, if you want to judge an effect).

The same room can provide you with many different subjects, if you focus your attention on a different aspect of it for each collage. A very simple way of isolating details from their surroundings is to look through a cardboard tube (such as a paper towel roll). The corner of a table, a bit of curtain, part of an object, suddenly fill your entire field of vision, suggesting compositions you never noticed before. You can translate these into exciting collages.

Fig. 16 Student, Hornsey College of Art: cut-paper collage from the model.

**Experiment 3**

This is a paper version of the mural technique known as 'sgraffito' (where a design is scratched or scraped through a ground of variously coloured layers of plaster). It is best suited to flat, decorative or abstract designs.

1 Take four sheets of fairly heavy paper or cardboard, of various textures (in fig. 17, smooth white cardboard was used for the top layer, rough sandpaper for the second layer, emery paper for the third, and corrugated cardboard for the bottom layer). Cut the sheets to the same size as the support they are to be mounted on.

2 Draw a simple design on the sheet you wish to use as the top layer (these are the principal shapes, which the subsequent layers will 'fill in' with other, smaller shapes). With a stencil knife or other suitable tool, go round the edges of your design and cut away the shapes (fig. 18).

3 Place this top sheet over the one which is to be the second layer (fig. 19), and draw another set of shapes to fit within the contours of the first. Now cut these away, so that you have more 'holes' to be filled (fig. 20).

4 Continue in this manner until your design is complete, and you have exposed parts of each different texture.

5 Finally, glue the bottom layer down to your support and the other layers one over the other, in their proper sequence (fig. 21).

You can accentuate the relief, if you wish, by using more layers of cardboard.

Try the same experiment using magazine pages for one or more of the layers, alternating them with plain coloured paper or cardboard. Many variations will undoubtedly occur to you; you might use photographs, pieces of cloth, small objects, etc., on some layers.

There is no limit to the variety of shapes, colours and patterns which can be superimposed one over the other in this way, creating an extraordinarily rich effect.

If you want to try this technique on realistic subjects, make some sketches from landscape and still-life, treating everything as 'shapes within shapes' (it may help you to think of the patterns on Oriental carpets).

As you can see from the examples on the following pages, cut-outs can be used in many different ways to express ideas,

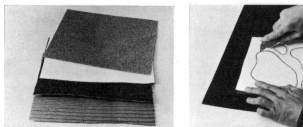

Fig. 17

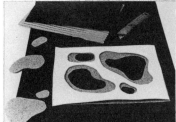

Fig. 18

Fig. 19

Fig. 20

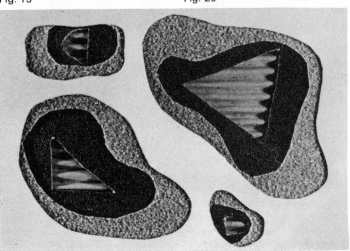

Fig. 21 Finished work.

suggest moods and describe visual impressions.

Perhaps you have a cherished theme, something you have always wanted to illustrate: take it as the starting point for a series of collages, limiting yourself to only one aspect of the idea per panel. Don't give up too soon if something doesn't turn out as you expected; the right idea and the right technique rarely find each other at once. When they do, you know immediately that all your 'failed' attempts were not failures at all, but necessary steps in the realization of your idea.

Rather than rely on subjects that are generally supposed to be inspiring to artists (sunsets, etc.), try to find out what it is that really moves and stimulates you personally. What inspiration consists of is different things to different people, but I think we can all agree on what it 'feels like' to be inspired. Start with this genuine excitement, stay with it, and you will always produce more interesting and original work than if you borrow others' moods and ideas.

Fig. 22 Student, Camden Arts Centre: *The Vista*. Cut paper (photographs, illustrations, type, coloured paper).

Fig. 23 Aubrey Williams: collage of painted paper.

Paper which you tone or paint yourself, then cut up into various shapes, is a way of using collage as an extension of painting. If you have a pile of your own sketches and studies stored away somewhere, try cutting up some of them and assembling the pieces into new compositions, perhaps adding other elements, printed paper, etc.

An exploration of second-hand bookshops, local bazaars and auctions, might provide you with a rich stock of prints, engravings, etc., which could be just right for some of your collages.

Figs. 24, 25 Sauro Bertelli. *London* and *New York* collages. 1967 Alitalia calendar. Courtesy of Alitalia Italian Airlines.

26

Fig. 26 John Christoferson: *Constellations*. Cut-paper collage. Courtesy of Leicester Galleries, London.

**Experiment 4**

Photomontage, or the assembling of photographs into new backgrounds and combinations, has been practised since at least the middle of the nineteenth century (see p. 85). This process is either carried out in the darkroom (by combining negatives, etc.), or simply by cutting out photographs from various sources, arranging them and pasting them down so that they seem to merge together.

1 Select a title for your collage. (Perhaps a line of poetry or a phrase chosen at random from a book).

2 Go through all your magazines and cut out those photographs which have some relation, however remote, to your theme. Try limiting yourself to black and white pictures, or else only to colour pictures.

3 Cut out only those parts of a photograph which are relevant to your subject (for example, in a figure, it may be just the hand that you need).

4 Put all your cut-outs down on the background to which they are going to be pasted (this might be another photograph, mounted on a hard surface), and combine them in any manner you wish. Fantasy and optical illusion are the main elements of photomontage; try to blend edges and tones together so that one cannot tell where the different photographs are joined.

Fig. 27 Making the montage.

Fig. 28 Finished work.

Fig. 29 Jack Yates: *Coming and Going.* Photomontage.

Fig. 30 Hans Schwarz: photomontage.

Fig. 31 Walz-Katzenstein: *La Mamma*. Photomontage.

# 4 Torn-paper collage

A shape whose edges are torn has a totally different character to one that has been cut: it seems to have just 'happened'. You can use this accidental quality on its own, or combine it with more controlled techniques.

Perhaps the most striking examples of the way in which accidental processes can suggest or resemble creative processes can be seen in torn hoardings (billboards). The next experiment describes a technique basically the same as that which produces these accidental effects, often surprisingly stimulating to the imagination.

Fig. 32 Torn posters.

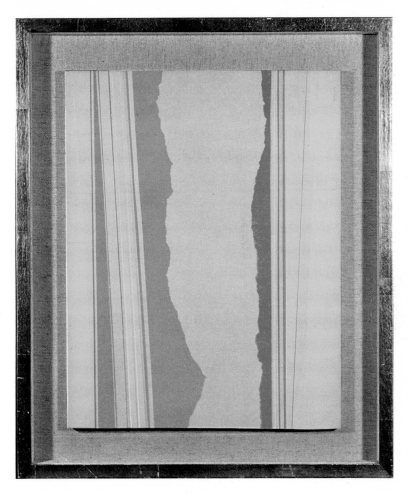

Fig. 33 Bernard Gay: torn and cut-paper collage.

Fig. 34

Fig. 35

Fig. 36

Fig. 37 Finished work.

34

## Experiment 1

The following technique is known as 'décollage' (ungluing). It consists basically of pasting several layers of paper one over the the other, then gradually removing parts of each layer. (It is another variation on the 'sgraffito' experiment described on p. 22.)

1 Cut four or more sheets of paper to the same size as the surface on which they are to be mounted. You can use coloured paper, or tone the sheets yourself with poster colours, acrylic colours, etc.

2 Before gluing the sheets down, decide on the order that the colours should appear; try one colour next to another and see whether you prefer sudden contrasts or a gradual progression of tones. Paste the bottom sheet to the support, and then the next layers one over the other (fig. 34), allowing each sheet to dry under pressure for a few minutes before pasting the next one. The paper may wrinkle slightly, but this is of no importance.

3 Begin by moistening a small area of the top sheet with a water-filled brush. Then peel the paper away (fig. 35), letting the torn edges form a shape, exposing the first colour underneath.

4 Continue moistening and tearing through to the other layers (fig. 36), allowing the design to suggest itself and controlling it wherever necessary. If you feel that too much white shows at the frayed edges, you can tone these with colour, or smoke them with a candle. Hold the picture upside down over a candle flame, allowing the smoke to blacken the area. It is difficult to restrict this process to small areas, but you can rub off unwanted soot with the fingers. A fixative or varnish should be applied to the finished work.

Try the same experiment using magazine covers instead of, or combined with, coloured papers. Thin cardboard may also be used (cereal boxes are good), and other possibilities include wallpaper, old paperback-book covers, calendars, posters of all kinds. Black and white photographs on hard, glossy paper also lend themselves very well to this technique.

You could incorporate areas of décollage in some of your compositions of cut-paper or you could prepare several décollage backgrounds to serve as a base for various subjects.

The weathered, 'aged', look that such backgrounds often have, especially if many layers of different kinds have been superimposed, can be accentuated by the application of one or several washes of thin colour (watercolour, acrylic, or oil colours), allowed to run into the edges and creases of the paper. A rough wooden plank or board would make a good support, with parts of the wood grain allowed to show.

If you want to work from a predetermined design, draw it lightly on the top sheet and use a stencil knife to score the outlines before you begin tearing.

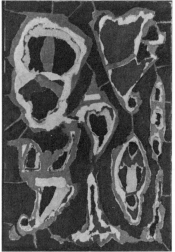

Figs. 38, 39 Students, Camden Arts Centre: décollage experiments.

Fig. 40 Jack Yates: *Slim.* Torn paper.

## Experiment 2

Torn paper provides an ideal medium with which to explore the principles of composition and basic design. A good idea alone is not sufficient without understanding of these principles, and even accidental effects must go through a process of selection before you accept them as indispensable elements in your work.

1  Choose a few sheets of paper of various textures and tones (fig. 41).
2  Tear them into rectangles of different sizes (fig. 42).
3  Use some of these pieces to make an abstract composition. You may find that the edges look better if they are not pasted down flat but allowed to curl up: in that case, glue only the centre of the shape to the support, and leave the edges of the paper free.
4  Continue making these arrangements of torn paper until you have a sequence of them, almost like a musical composition, each part able to stand on its own, but also related to the whole (figs. 43, 44).

When arranging furniture in a room, you take into consideration the amount of space available, the shape of your furniture, the colours that 'go together' and the use you will make of the room. Roughly the same principles apply to creating a satisfying abstract composition as go into making an 'atmosphere' in which to live. Perhaps you find it difficult to see the 'usefulness' of an abstract picture, whereas a room's function is quite obvious. However, you will undoubtedly agree that the atmosphere of different people's houses varies tremendously, even though they might be identical from a functional point of view: it is this indefinable 'atmosphere' which your experiments in abstract composition help you to convey.

Try some compositions using only letters, words, or numbers torn from newspapers and magazines. Watercolour paper, crumpled tissue-paper and oriental papers offer many possibilities of texture and have beautiful edges when torn.

Another way to create irregular edges is by burning: simply hold a match or candle to your paper (it is wise to do this standing over a sink), and blow out or douse the flame when you have the sort of edges you want. Parts of collages which have already been pasted down may also be given this burnt effect by touching them quickly with a flame.

Fig. 41

Fig. 42

Fig. 43

Fig. 44

## Experiment 3

Torn-paper 'mosaics' are a delightful way of making abstract compositions or of working from life, creating surfaces that seem to vibrate, due to the infinite, small variations of colour.

Simply tear a few sheets of any type of coloured or printed paper into small pieces of various sizes, and use these to 'build up' your picture without doing any preliminary drawing. Paste them down as you go, overlapping edges, working boldly and quickly.

The example shown in fig. 47 was done in black, grey and white paper, using a reproduction of Correggio's *Madonna of St. Girolamo* as a model and interpreting it freely.

Fig. 45 Student, Hornsey College of Art: torn and cut-paper collage from the model.

Fig. 46 Student, Camden Arts Centre: coloured tissue paper mosaic.

Fig. 47 Student, Camden Arts Centre: black, grey and white paper mosaic.

## Experiment 4

A project which could be very absorbing and to which you might devote a considerable amount of time is a collage 'autobiography'.

You will have no difficulty, I am sure, in finding a great number of odds and ends which have some special significance for you: old letters and envelopes, snapshots, postcards, tickets, newspaper clippings, souvenirs of all sorts. Collage comes naturally to the diary and scrapbook 'addicts', who will find that they already have on hand enough material for a whole series of collages.

Putting all this material together so that it is visually interesting is by no means an easy matter. Just pasting one scrap next to another can sometimes produce an exciting result, if you are lucky; on the other hand, it can also end in a confused clutter. There is no recipe for arriving at a successful collage; try to achieve a balance between chance effects and planning. Your previous experiments will have helped you to do this.

When you have gathered all your memorabilia, decide on the general form you want to give your 'autobiography'. For example, it could be one large panel, or a series of small panels; or a collage in book-form.

Torn edges can be contrasted with cut-out shapes; you can try combining or adapting all the techniques you have experimented with so far.

Fig. 48
Jack Yates: mirror collage.

# 5 Fabric collage

The profusion of colours, textures and patterns available in cloth make it a wonderful collage material, providing you resist the temptation of simply using the designs on the fabric instead of your own ideas. Cloth has very personal, emotional associations which do not lose their character even when the fabrics are used in an abstract way, perhaps because cloth always seems to invite the touch. This tactile quality could provide the stimulus for many of your experiments using fabrics.

Making a collage from fabrics does not differ essentially from making one from paper, and most of the experiments suggested in this book can be adapted to include or make exclusive use of cloth, taking into consideration its particular characteristics: cloth can be stretched tight, or draped, padded, allowed to hang loosely, stitched, stiffened; its edges can be neatly cut, or frayed, ravelled, ripped, burnt. Light plays an important part: some fabrics (such as silks, satins, rayons, lamés, taffetas, plastics, or leather) reflect light, glistening softly or sparkling boldly. Others, like velvet, hessian (burlap), brocade, etc., absorb light and seem to have a 'deep', sonorous tone. Transparent or fragile materials (lace, chiffon, or organdie) immediately introduce a whimsical mood. Any mood, in fact, can be conjured up by some type of fabric.

A good beginning to your experiments with fabrics would be to decide on a mood or tactile sensation (e.g., rough, smooth, cool or warm) which you want to express, and then set about finding suitable materials. Alternatively, you could look over all the scraps and remnants of cloth that you have on hand, and see what they suggest to you.

The contact adhesives (Evo-Stik, Weldwood) are suitable for cloth, and craft supply shops also stock a variety of special glues for leather, plastic, etc. Supports for fabric collages are the same as those mentioned on p. 14, with the emphasis on the fact that they should be rigid. You can also use empty frames or stretchers, tacking your fabrics to the edges and gluing other pieces of cloth on top. A useful item to have is a round weaving needle (with a turned up point), or any similar tool, for pulling out threads from woven fabrics. (The open patterns on the fabric-hanging in fig. 55 were made in this way.) Straw matting, string, and all kinds of rope might come in handy, as well as old gloves, discarded handbags, belts, hats, and so on.

Whether you use fabrics to make abstract compositions, interpret what you see, or give free rein to your imagination, you must remember that the materials you use have a very strong 'presence' of their own, which will, to some extent, influence your idea. In order to understand this point, I suggest you try a simple exercise.

Draw a stylized shape or symbol (for example, the sun), and cut it out of several kinds of fabric. You will see immediately that a 'velvet sun' has a totally different character to, say, a 'tweed sun' or a 'flowered print sun'. If you now make as many fabric collages as you have 'suns', choosing your other pieces of material to complement each mood, you will begin to realize some of the possibilities and problems of creating with fabrics.

The examples on the following pages show you some of the exciting results achieved by artists who have explored this medium and adapted it to their own ends.

Fig. 49 Student, Camden Arts Centre: fabric collage.

Fig. 50 Enrico Baj: *Lady Sensitive to the Weather*. Fabrics, thermometer, beads, braiding, etc. First prize winner of 1966 Ascher Award Competition. Courtesy Ascher (London) Limited.

Fig. 51 William Copley: *Suitable for Framing*. Fabrics. Courtesy Ascher (London) Limited.

Printed fabrics offer the element of repetition which is nearly always present in decorative art. In fact, it is difficult *not* to produce something decorative when using repeat patterns, whether you draw those patterns yourself or borrow them from fabrics. It would be a challenge to your creative ingenuity to invent ways in which you could incorporate repetition in some of your collages, without letting it dominate your ideas.

You may have asked yourself, what is it that makes one work 'decoration' and another one 'art'? I can only venture an answer by suggesting another experiment.

Fig. 52 June Tiley: *Disintegrated Circle, red, white and blue.* Fabrics.
Courtesy Ascher (London) Limited.

Give yourself a decorative assignment (e.g., making a fabric-collage screen for your living-room). You can carry out this project adopting the 'decorator's' point of view, using colours and patterns which will blend in perfectly with the existing arrangement of the room. Or, you might begin with this end in mind, and then discover during the process of making the screen that you are going off on some other tangent altogether, and would have to rearrange the room to go with your screen—which may not end up as a screen after all!

Such experiments could help you to see for yourself the results produced by different creative attitudes.

If painting is of major interest to you, you will find that fabrics can be used as though they were simply another type of pigment, and can also be combined with traditional artists' media; here is a brief list of some processes you might try.

Primed artists' canvas, cut or torn into pieces, dipped in oil paint (slightly liquified by mixing with linseed oil and a little turpentine), allowed to dry, and then used as collage materials.

Unprimed canvas, edges burnt, used in collages.

Holes made in a canvas by cutting, tearing, or burning; other materials glued behind the holes.

Discarded paintings cut up into sections and used in collages.

Different types of fabrics tacked to a wooden stretcher and pulled tight; other cloth glued on top, or 'woven' in between.

A wire-mesh base for making a 'woven collage', using various pieces of cloth, string, or small objects.

Thin cloth glued to a wooden base and manipulated into ridges and wrinkles before the glue dries.

Coarse canvas, stiffened with glue sizing, cut up and used to make collages in which the shapes, only partially pasted to the base, are allowed to stand up in relief.

Fabric reliefs in which surfaces are built up by pasting layers of cloth one over the other.

'Decalcomania': oil paint spread in the centre of two sheets of canvas, the two pressed together then peeled apart, revealing strange, symmetrical designs. These, in turn, can be elaborated, or cut out and used as is in collages.

Transparent fabrics, glued over paper or other materials.

Cloth, dipped in plaster of Paris, can be molded into shapes before the plaster hardens. These 'solid folds' can then be glued to a rigid surface and combined with other elements. (The plaster is prepared as follows: sieve a fine stream of plaster of Paris through your fingers into a bowl half full of water. Stir the mixture with your hands until it feels smooth and free from lumps, and about the consistency of cream. It must now be used at once, as it begins to harden very quickly.)

I hope that I have not given you the impression that decorative aims are to be disregarded. There is as much scope for creativity in the field of applied art as there is in 'fine' art, and the surroundings in which you live would undoubtedly benefit from your experimenting with the decorative possibilities of fabric collage.

Perhaps as you look around you at this moment, you can see several projects that you might undertake; here are two examples.

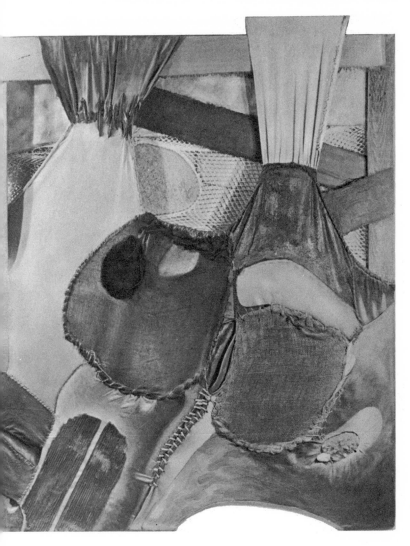

Fig. 53 Edward Bullmore: *Hikurangi No. 9*. Painted canvas, hessian, and other fabrics, string stitching, padding, wood.

## A fabric collage room-divider

Measure the space you want the divider to occupy; decide whether it is a permanent fixture, or a movable one. If it is to be permanent, you could build a rigid wooden frame, attached to floor and ceiling, upon which to stretch the fabric. Or, if you are going to use a stiff fabric as a base for the collage, you could simply tack it to a strip of wood at the top and let it hang in Japanese-scroll fashion, weighting the bottom with another strip of wood inserted in the hem. Straw matting or a length of bamboo curtain would be effective, hung in this manner.

An old screen, or a bookshelf of the right dimensions, could provide the support for a movable divider. (On the shelf-side of the bookcase, the collage would serve as a background for pottery, etc. Or, the base fabric could be tacked to both sides, hiding the shelves completely.)

As the screen will be viewed from both sides, you can take advantage of light effects when planning your design. Holes can be cut out of the base fabric, the edges ravelled or stitched. Pieces of string, or hemp, can be 'woven' into the base fabric, in abstract patterns; paper and other materials can also be incorporated in the design and glued to the base.

## A fabric collage mural

A fabric 'mural' for a child's room (or any other room) is another possible project. An area of faded or stained wallpaper which you want to cover could serve as a base (providing the wall is dry). Wall surfaces to which fabrics or other materials are to be pasted should always be dry and in good condition; it is preferable to prime or size the wall first: the polymer-acrylic products include white primers (e.g., Cryla primer, Polymer primer), which dry rapidly and can be applied directly to plaster or masonry.

Fig. 54 Gerard Dillon: *The Beast-Bird*. Oil and piece of an old crocodile handbag. Collection of Sir Basil Goulding.

The powers of suggestion which fabrics possess are extraordinary, and articles of old clothing, in particular, are rich in associations (often nostalgic or macabre, related as they are to the past, to age and decay). Fragments of used clothing, found in second-hand stores and market stalls, can assume new life, when transformed by the imagination of the collagist.

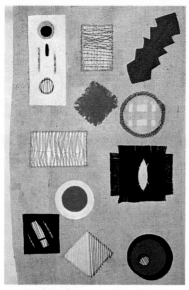

Fig. 55 Blanche d'Arbeloff: fabric hanging.

Fig. 56 Noreen Rice: leather on carved and painted wood.

Fig. 57 Edward Bullmore: *Hikurangi*, 1963.

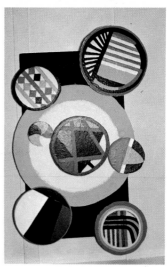

Fig. 58 Student: assemblage.

Fig. 59 Wojciech Sadley: *Old Man*. Sisal, bamboo, linen. Courtesy Grabowski Gallery, London (from 1966 exhibition of contemporary Polish tapestries).

Fig. 60 Jack Yates: *People*. Matchboxes, plastic emulsion paints, mono-type, small objects, and paper cut-outs. Courtesy William Ware Gallery, London.

# 6 Mixed media

'You may paint with whatever material you like—with pipes, postage stamps and playing cards, candelabra, pieces of cloth, collars, painted paper, newspapers.' Apollinaire, 1913.

It is not an exaggeration to state that any material and any technique can be used in collage. A complete description of methods would therefore have to include all the traditional art and craft techniques: oil painting, watercolour painting, tempera painting, etching, engraving, wood-cuts, lino-cuts, sculpture, etc. This is obviously not within the scope of this book; I have described a few of the more unorthodox creative techniques evolved by artists through trial and error, in the hope that you will be encouraged to develop variations on them, as well as to invent new methods of your own.

A few words about equipment: the acrylic-polymer colours mentioned on p. 14 are particularly versatile for use with collage. As these colours dry very quickly, it is advisable to keep them moist while working (a small plastic squeeze-bottle makes a handy spray). Colour should not be allowed to dry on brushes or tools, which should be thoroughly rinsed in water after use. The acrylic primers are also useful: they can be applied without dilution to paper, cardboard, plastic, wood, fabrics, or canvas prior to painting on the surface with acrylic colours. Relief textures can be built up with the colours themselves, applied with a palette knife, or with special 'Texture paste' (see p. 56).

Oil colours can be effectively combined with collage, used in 'glazes' (thinned with linseed oil) or thickly applied. Household emulsion paints, enamels, lacquers, plastic paints, varnishes, stains, etc., can all be used and experimented with.

Black Indian ink can be used in a great variety of ways: spread over a coloured wax-crayon drawing and allowed to dry, it can then be scraped away in places, making an interesting mottled texture. Waterproof coloured inks, watercolours, poster colours, gouache (opaque watercolour) and crayons are good to have on hand. Soft sable or squirrel brushes should be used with water-based paints; the stiff bristle brushes are better for oils.

## Experiment 1: imprints

Natural imprints are everywhere to be seen: footprints in the sand, tyre tracks in the mud, etc.

This method makes use of the same natural process: you press objects into a soft, malleable surface, then take them away, leaving their 'imprints'.

1. You will need the following: a rigid support; any quick-setting preparation capable of registering and retaining imprints, and which will not crack or pull away from the surface when dry. (Rowney Cryla Texture Paste was used for this experiment.) Plaster of Paris is also suitable: mix as directed on p. 48, pour onto a sheet of hardboard (Masonite), rough side up, around which you have built an inch-high 'wall' of plasticine or clay; proceed as below, removing the objects only when the plaster has thoroughly set.

2. If you are using a preparation in paste form, spread it thickly onto your support with a palette knife (fig. 61).

3. Allow the surface to dry partially (until your finger leaves a clear mark when pressed onto it), then press small objects or textures into it (fig. 62).

4. When the surface is dry, remove the objects. You can now add collage elements, if you wish (fig. 63), using a fresh application of Texture Paste as an adhesive.

5. Add colour, if desired, in thin washes, brushed into the crevices to bring out the design. Acrylic, oil or watercolours may be used (fig. 64).

6. Varnish the finished work with a matt acrylic or other varnish. (On a plaster base, shoe polish in different shades may be used instead of colour, to bring out the reliefs; also wood-stains.)

Many interesting variations on this technique will occur to you as you work. You will find that certain kinds of textures and shapes lend themselves to easy reproduction, while others are too indefinite or weak. Machine and clock parts are good; rough sacking, corrugated cardboard, embossed papers, sandpaper (sand itself can be imbedded in the surface), bits of metal and glass, bottle caps, small medicine bottles, costume jewelry, household utensils or tools, are other suggestions.

Fig. 61

Fig. 62

Fig. 63

Fig. 64

Fig. 65 Finished work.

## Experiment 2: aluminium foil rubbings

As you have undoubtedly noticed, kitchen foil molds itself to whatever it is pressed on. This quality can be exploited to make 'rubbings', which in turn can be used as collage elements.

Place the foil over any raised or textured surface, and press firmly with the hand, rubbing gently to insure a clear impression. A clothes-brush or hairbrush may be tapped gently over surfaces that are very intricate, so that the foil is pushed into all the interstices. String is particularly interesting: complex patterns can be made with it, then rubbings taken of them. The samples shown in fig. 66 were done from matchsticks, a string bag, scissors, a ceramic jug, string, an iron grating, and a chip-fryer.

Fig. 66 Samples of aluminium foil rubbings.

## Experiment 3: glass painting and collage

Paint, behind glass, takes on a distant, unreal appearance, suggesting many possibilities for experiment. Here is one method of combining painting on glass with collage.

One side of a sheet of glass is coated evenly with paint (the aerosol spray-paints are useful for this); household emulsion paints can also be used. A design, in outline only, is drawn on the surface when dry; the shapes inside the contours are scraped away, and selected papers (magazine cut-outs, etc.) pasted on the glass, face down, over the 'open' areas.

Many variations are possible, using various layers of paper behind glass, in the 'décollage' technique (p. 35).

Fig. 67 Hansi Bohm: collage and painting on glass.

## Experiment 4: reverse printing

You can take a reversed impression of newsprint in the following manner.

Coat one side of a sheet of smooth (not glossy) paper with wax: white wax crayon, neutral shoe-cream, candle-wax, etc. (lighter fuel also works). Place the waxed side over the part of the newspaper you wish to use (it must be *newsprint*, magazine paper will not transfer). Rub the back of the paper with a burnisher or spoon (fig. 68), taking care to go over the entire surface in a circular motion, so as to avoid streaks. Lift the paper, and there you have a reversed image of the newsprint (fig. 69), which you can paste into a collage, or use as a base for a collage.

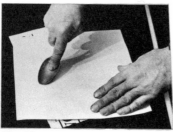
Fig. 68

Fig. 69

Fig. 70 Natalie d'Arbeloff: reverse printing and collage.

The example in fig. 70 was done as follows.

The paper was waxed with white wax crayon. Transfers were taken from typeset words and phrases of gradually decreasing sizes (to create distance). The figures were cut out, and arranged on the paper, also in decreasing sizes. The same figures were used several times for transfers, and finally the cut-outs themselves were pasted next to their shadowy 'doubles'.

Fig. 71 Gerard Dillon: *The Money-Bird's Dead*. Oil and collage of coins. Patrick Hickey Collection.

The use of collage in combination with painting is a vast field in itself. Some of the ways in which the techniques are used fall into distinct categories, others are impossible to pin down.

The *trompe l'oeil* (fool the eye) tradition would, as applied to collage, be the use of materials as 'themselves'. For example, gluing a real shell to a board and painting a realistic beach around it.

Another approach consists of arranging collage materials to form a design, and adding painted details which make the design 'become' something else. For example, buttons and screws assembled together and transformed into a face by the addition of painted hair and eyes.

Collage elements can also be introduced in a painting for their personal associations, as part of the picture's subject-matter.

Finally, paper or other collage materials can be used simply as another type of 'pigment', in combination with oil or other media, to achieve certain textural effects. Cut or torn-paper shapes can be introduced in a painting, for their interest as pattern and colour, and for the 'shock' of their juxtaposition with painted areas.

Fig. 72 Natalie d'Arbeloff: *Variations on an Underground theme*. Oil and collage of own drawings, etchings, and a magazine cut-out.

Fig. 73 Jack Yates: *Winning Hand.* Oil, monotype and collage.

Fig. 74 Peter Paone: *Study for Carnaby Street.* Gouache and collage.

64

Fig. 75 F. N. Souza: *Portrait of Mr. and Mrs. Oswald Jones.* Gouache and collage of photographs.

Fig. 76 Max Chapman: *Collage noyé*. Paper, emulsions, and oil.

Fig. 77 Tony Underhill: *August 22, 1966.* Oil and collage. Courtesy Hamilton Galleries, London.

Fig. 78 Jack Yates: *The General.* Assemblage of found objects on wood.

# 7 Assemblage

Assemblage is simply the extension of collage to include the use of any and all material objects of every description, size and weight.

Such unlimited choice can lead to total confusion. The process of 'assembling' attempts to make some order out of this confusion, by a process of association (very like the word-association game derived from psychology: someone gives you a word, you answer whatever comes into your mind at that moment).

The exploration of assemblage by artists in our century has largely done away with the dividing lines between painting, sculpture, construction, even light, sound, and movement, by combining all or some of them. How far you can go in this process is entirely up to you, and the techniques are to a great extent dependent on the materials you choose to assemble. The same applies to the equipment you will need: you might want a complete do-it-yourself workshop, with a variety of hammers, saws, drills, pliers, planes, tin-snips, glass-cutters, and so on; you may find that all you need is a good strong glue and a few basic tools.

Assemblages are not necessarily large or heavy: they may be made of nothing more than matchsticks and bottle caps. It is a good idea, however, to have on hand a strong, permanent, all-purpose adhesive, such as the contact glues or the most permanent of all, the epoxy resins such as Araldite, or the many comparable American epoxy cements.

Some other items which you might find useful are: wood-stains and varnishes; metallic paints; paints in aerosol spray cans; polyurethane varnish (for waterproofing wood, etc.); plaster of Paris; polyester resin (see the list for further reading for the title of a specialized work on the use of plastics).

The materials themselves that you can assemble can be roughly classified according to their availability to you, and the limitations of your time and your working-space. Through your work, or your friends and acquaintances, you may have access to excellent sources of materials which might not occur to you if you simply went out searching at random. It is not necessary to look far or to go to great expense: what is right at your fingertips may be exactly the material which will start you off on your assemblage experiments.

A few of the infinite number of possible materials for assemblage are:

Wood: crates, shingles, barrels, blocks, old doors, frames, parts of furniture, bread boards and draining boards, sticks and tree branches, ornamental mouldings, wooden toys.

Metal: tin cans, household hardware, old pots and pans, automobile and other machine parts, wheels, springs, electric fittings, pipes and plumbing fixtures, sheet metal.

Glass and ceramic: bottles, pieces of coloured glass, broken china, ceramic tiles, flower pots, bricks.

Miscellaneous: corks, scraps of plastic, formica, Perspex, (Plexiglas), celluloid, plastic kitchen utensils.

Although, strictly speaking, a 'pure' assemblage would be a construction of found parts (natural or manufactured) without any attempt to alter the parts themselves but simply relating them, the term has come to embrace so many variations that almost any structure in various parts can be said to be an assemblage. It would be impossible to establish any definite technique for making an assemblage; one can only describe individual experiences and make lists of the materials that artists have used for this purpose. In general, the 'assembling' process seems to arise out of a few basic attitudes.

1 Allowing the shape and character of the found object to suggest an idea, then elaborating or interpreting that idea in a personal way.

An example of this is Edward Bullmore's *Astroform No. 3* (fig. 79), which originated when the artist found a piece of curved wood among the discarded materials of a carpentry school. He explains that this shape immediately suggested a winged form to him, and he began to build another half to match his 'found object'; this was quite a complicated undertaking, and by the time the two 'wings' were ready, he had decided to put a male and a female torso between them: these he made by stretching canvas over a padded wooden base, then painting it.

The found object, in the final result, has been completely taken over by the artist's conception, and yet served as the springboard for it. (See also fig. 53, p. 49, and fig. 57, p. 52.) Edward Bullmore is a New Zealander, working in London.

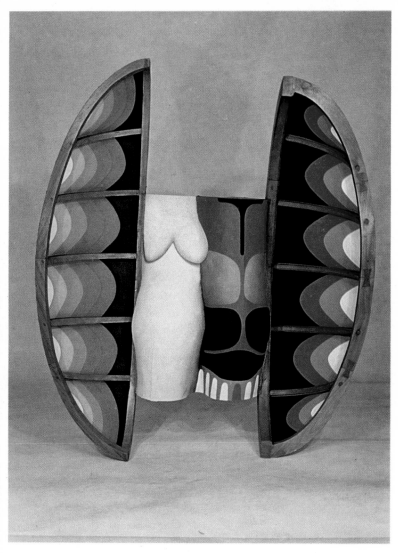

Fig. 79 Edward Bullmore: *Astroform No. 3.* Found wood, painted canvas and padding. Courtesy Tama Gallery, London.

71

Fig. 80 Student, Camden Arts Centre: assemblage of found objects.

Fig. 81 Student, Camden Arts Centre: assemblage of boxes, etc.

2 Putting found objects together and finding relationships between them.

The collecting of found objects is already halfway to the creating of an assemblage: you pick up certain things and reject others, drawn by indefinable qualities which correspond to something in yourself. When you spread the materials out before you, they are already, in a sense, 'related' by the fact of your having chosen them.

The examples shown in figs. 80 and 81 were done by students who had been asked to bring any odds and ends they could find, and to make an assemblage of them. The support was wood, hardboard or cardboard, coated with 'Polyfilla', a cellulose preparation used to patch cracks in plaster walls. This type of preparation may be used for experiments, but tends to flake off when applied thickly or on other surfaces than those it is intended for.

Openings were cut out of the support in both examples, and objects inserted and fastened in these 'niches': egg-cartons, boxes, etc. String was stretched over the central opening in fig. 80, behind which is a box containing various small objects.

The American artist Louise Nevelson works with boxes of many shapes and sizes which she arranges into compartmented structures; into these she assembles wooden objects: newel posts, arms, seats and backs of chairs, table-legs, discs and cylinders, patterned moulding, etc., in carefully balanced, geometric compositions. The final result is sometimes sprayed with gilt paint.

3 Giving new meanings to familar objects.

Noreen Rice, (whose *Skipping Figure* is shown in fig. 82), is an Irish artist working in London, who creates what she calls 'figurative abstracts' from found objects of familiar domestic use, such as locks and keys, weighing scales, gas cooker and sewing machine parts, utensils and tools, gloves and shoes. She generally mounts the pieces on wood by screwing them into place (most of her assemblages are 'dismountable'), rather than gluing them; when leather, etc., is used, she employs strong adhesives to fix them down. Decorative motifs are sometimes burned onto the wooden base (see fig. 56).

The base for the *Skipping Figure* is the flap-top of a sewing machine; the body of the figure, a broken sieve (the handle representing the legs in motion). The head is made from a bicycle lamp; the nose is the bulb of the lamp. Three screws hold the parts together, two of them serving as the eyes of the figure.

Among assemblages by Noreen Rice is also a *Crucifix,* fashioned from crushed wire-mesh, the body of cast iron, a butcher's hook and wire cages, the feet suggested by a big corroded spoon.

Miro (the Spanish artist, associated with the Surrealist movement, see p. 94), created an assemblage in 1936 which he entitled *Objet poetique;* it is a kind of 'tower', the base of which is a man's hat. The middle section is an oval wooden frame (inside which is suspended a 'leg' made of a padded stocking inside a real shoe), and the 'top storey' consists of a stuffed parrot sitting on an artificial branch, from which hangs a ball on a string: a paper map of the world and a small toy fish complete the structure.

Joseph Cornell, the American artist who began making his 'boxes' in the early 1930's, has had a strong influence on present day assemblage. He puts together various objects inside wooden boxes, giving them a mysterious, timeless quality. Some of the objects he has thus 'immortalized' include astrological and astronomical maps, apothecary jars, old photographs and prints, starfish, jewelry and dials.

'Readymades' (or ordinary objects presented 'as is, with little or no attempt to alter them) were first proposed to a shocked and skeptical public in 1913 by Marcel Duchamp, a forerunner of the Dada movement (see p. 88), who exhibited a bicycle wheel fastened to a wooden stool.

74

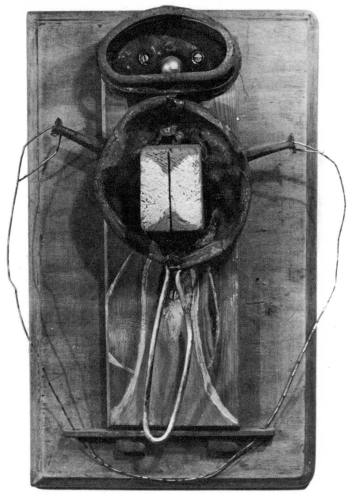

Fig. 82 Noreen Rice: *Skipping Figure*. Assemblage.

4 Beginning with a specific idea in mind, finding appropriate objects, then combining the idea with those objects.

An example of this is the assemblage *Ramona* (fig. 83). The initial idea was evolved from sketches in which single words enclosed in rectangles were used as elements of composition. I tried this with the words of the song 'Ramona', but was not satisfied with the result as a drawing: it was only when finding by chance a dozen or so small, rough, wooden blocks (some of them perforated), that I realized the way in which I wanted to execute my idea. I glued some of the blocks down to a piece of hardboard (Masonite), and arranged them in a similar manner as in my original sketches. The perforations served as the 'o's for the words 'Ramona' and 'gone' and for a little window in the centre. The rough, cross-grain surface of the blocks provided an interesting texture, which I accentuated by painting curves on some areas. The words of the song provided the images, which in turn suggested to me a particular kind of landscape, tropical and wild; I found some old snapshots of South America which I cut up and glued on parts of the base, and on some sides of the blocks. The images on the blocks were painted with Cryla colours, and the base with black plastic enamel. Finally, the blocks were given several coats of acrylic varnish.

The categories I have used to describe the process of assemblage are by no means the only ways in which to approach the subject, but I hope they will be of some help in getting you started on this fascinating and unpredictable creative activity.

You will find that one thing really does lead to another: ideas are generated by materials, materials animated by ideas.

If you have any furniture you want to get rid of, a project you might undertake would be to transform the unwanted item into a piece of 'fantasy furniture', taking parts away, adding other parts, painting, scraping, pasting and constructing until something (or someone!) says 'Stop'.

Assemblages can also be made from parts which you yourself have constructed or painted. Such an example is fig. 58 by an adult student, entitled *Planets*. The shapes painted within the circles resulted from an exercise in which the class was asked to examine the room, looking through cardboard tubes (see p. 20), and to paint the shapes thus isolated and selected. This produced very interesting, boldly coloured and simplified shapes, which this

Fig. 83 Natalie d'Arbeloff: *Ramona.* Assemblage.

student later cut out, and pasted to polystyrene (cut into circles of various dimensions). She then mounted the circles to a base, on different levels built up from behind with spools, etc.

We live in an age of assemblage; modern mass-production methods turn out objects and parts of objects in a continuous flow, and slightly used articles are replaced almost instantly by new ones. This contributes to the making of an enormous scrap heap, which the artists of this century have been quick to investigate and see as potential collage and assemblage material.

The sculptures of Richard Stankiewicz (U.S.A.) are 'collages' welded together from junk, scrap iron, discarded machinery, broken castings. American Robert Rauschenberg's 'Combines' are painting-sculpture-collage-environment-constructions, including objects such as doors, pillows, stuffed animals, buckets and clothes. John Chamberlain (U.S.A.) assembles crushed automobile bodies, fenders, etc., retaining their bright lacquer colours. Daniel Spoerri (Swiss working in Paris) makes 'snare pictures'; assemblages consisting of objects such as a table and chair placed vertically and glued to a rigid support. The table-top, facing the spectator, is laid for breakfast, in fact the breakfast has already been eaten, as the cigarette butts, eggshells, empty milk container attest to, fixed there, immobilized forever. In France, Fernandez Arman has made assemblages of forks and spoons in a glass-covered box, of dolls' hands glued in a wooden drawer. John Latham (British) uses books, cut, torn and burned, as his assemblage-materials, mounting them on doors or other surfaces, combined with paint.

Even human beings are used as 'artists materials': Yves Klein (French) mixed colours which his models lathered themselves with, then directed them to 'print themselves' on blank canvases. In another experiment, Klein brushed auras around models as they lay face down on canvases.

We are becoming familiar with 'happenings' in which anything (or nothing) can happen, and in which both the participants and the spectators are 'assembled', juggled around, disguised, used as objects, transformed by light effects: this is 'collage' stepping into the domain of the theatre, and into psychology. It is 'action collage' (another aspect of which consists of works which the spectator is encouraged to re-arrange); this is not really a subject which a How-To-Do-It handbook can deal with. How to make an 'action collage' has only been described, to my knowledge, in a rather irreverent old English music-hall song, a verse of which I would like to quote in conclusion.

Father papered the parlour
You couldn't see him for paste
Dabbin' it here, dabbin' it there,
Paste and paper everywhere,
Mother was stuck to the ceiling
The kids were stuck to the floor,
I never seen a bloomin' family
So stuck up before.

(Author unknown)

Fig. 84

Fig. 85 Warrior's shield from Borneo, decorated with the hair of slain enemies. Courtesy Cambridge University Museum of Archaeology and Ethnology.

# 8 Historical background

It is only in the last fifty-odd years that the bits and pieces of which our everyday environment is composed have taken their place on the list of recognized 'artists' materials'.

Collage and its extensions could thus be considered a truly contemporary art form. Its roots, however, go as far back as mankind itself. Throughout history, people have been collecting, assembling, and fastening down fragments of the materials at hand, for purposes of decoration, amusement, or ritual. The primitive and folk art of every country and every period abounds with examples of ingenious 'collages', often remarkably similar to contemporary works.

The human body itself was probably the first 'support' for collage: primitive tribes have always decorated themselves with various materials, and the fashions of every era include examples of what might be called 'human collages'. The activity of 'dressing up' one's body or face with feathers, paint, masks, or elaborate head-dresses, is not unrelated to the activity of making collages and assemblages as we know them today.

Objects were the next surfaces to serve as supports for collage: primitive societies made use of hair, teeth, bones, skins, fur, and feathers, to adorn shields, masks, ritual and domestic objects. From about 3000 B.C., the Babylonian, Chaldean and Egyptian civilizations developed mosaic techniques to inlay various objects and musical instruments with minute pieces of lapis lazuli, mother of pearl, and other stones. The isolated civilizations of Central and South America (Inca, Maya, Aztec) used a primitive gum or sometimes pitch to stick tiny pieces of shell, gold, obsidian, turquoise, to their jewelry and other objects, in rich, intricate designs.

Other civilizations made use of the technique of mosaic: about 2000 B.C., the Minoans in Crete used stones and pebbles in different patterns and colours on their pavements. The Romans (from 800 B.C.) were the first to use mosaics on a large scale, on roads, city squares and walls. The golden age of mosaic was reached during the early Christian period in Southern Italy and the Byzantine period in Asia Minor. From 326 A.D. to 1453, Byzantine art flourished, producing the most magnificent examples of mosaic allied to architecture (e.g., the sixth-century church of St. Apollinare Nuova at Ravenna, Italy). Byzantine icons (religious images) on wood often have real jewels attached to the painted halos, crowns, costumes and backgrounds. Examples of this kind can also be found in Italian art of the fourteenth and fifteenth centuries, such as Crivelli's *Madonna and Child with Four Saints* (Brera Gallery, Milan), in which St. Peter carries a replica of a large gold key hanging on a real cord.

In the Far East, the history of collage is as old as that of paper: by 700 A.D., the Chinese were mounting scroll paintings on backgrounds of many layers of paper, to insure the elasticity of the scrolls. Using adhesives whose formulas were guild secrets, papers made from rice stalks, bamboo, hemp, cotton, and silk were superimposed in a traditional order, requiring great time and patience. In Japan, there are examples of pasted papers used as a background for calligraphy dating from the tenth century.

The *trompe l'oeil* (fool the eye) tradition of sixteenth and seventeenth-century Dutch and Flemish painting strongly influenced subsequent developments. In the seventeenth century, real butterflies were sometimes glued into a still-life, painted with such extraordinary skill that the painted flowers and objects seem more real than the real butterfly.

In the nineteenth and early twentieth centuries, artists in Europe and America were producing *trompe l'oeil* pictures that seem to be modern collages, until one realizes that the woodgrain, newspaper, postage stamps, lottery ticket or envelope, 'stuck' to the surface are actually painted illusions: such an example is John Haberle's *The Changes of Time* (1888). Other artists who worked in this tradition include Raphael Peale, William Harnett, John Peto and Jean Dubreuil. The works of these artists, and of others in the *trompe l'oeil* school, were widely distributed through remarkably faithful coloured lithograph reproductions, and enjoyed enormous popularity.

The Victorians were enthusiastic collagists. A popular pastime was the 'dressing up' of cheap prints (portraits of famous people, etc.) with bits of pasted-on finery. Book and catalogue illustrations, advertisements, visiting cards, bottle labels, and other paper mementos were carefully collected and kept in scrapbooks, or pasted on fire screens, furniture, glass bowls and dishes; they were also glued to soft muslin pages with hand-stitched edges, for home-made children's picture books. Victorian Valentines were often elaborate collages, as were their 'mourning pictures', decorated with flowers and trees made of human hair.

With the discovery of photography by Nicéphore Niepce in

France in 1826 (later developed by Daguerre and others), a revolutionary new element was added to the ever-growing list of potential collage materials: the faithful likeness of anything and everything that a camera could be placed in front of. About 1835, working independently, the Frenchman Hippolyte Bayard and the Englishman W. H. Fox Talbot produced the first paper negatives, enabling photographs to be reproduced. Subsequent improvements brought photographs within the reach of everyone; by the 1860's, people were collecting 'cartes de visite' (visiting-card sized portraits, an invention by A. A. Disderi), and amusing themselves by assembling them in elaborate albums. Extraordinary, often altar-like constructions were built to serve as frames for the early 'daguerreotypes' and photographs.

Picture postcards came into use by about 1870. An interesting statistic: a survey of the postcard industry during the period of 1898-1900 showed an annual production of 500 million, of which 450 million were views and 50 million imaginative subjects. These 'imaginative subjects' were among the first 'photomontages', forerunners of the Surrealist fantasies of about 25 years later.

The early 1900's saw at least three events of major significance: the popularization of photography, the vogue for primitive art, and

Fig. 86 Postcard, early 1900's. Courtesy Thames and Hudson, London.

the use of collage by a few major artists. These three events contributed to the development of totally new ways of thinking and seeing, generally referred to as 'modern art'. For about five hundred years, art had been primarily concerned with the representation of 'things as they look', and for the professional artist to use real materials and objects rather than their painted images was not only considered irrelevant but downright insulting to his profession. But the advent of photography, and the dissatisfaction of a few artists with the accepted canons of 'good taste', led to a re-examination of the role of the artist as a skilled reporter of reality. A vogue for the primitive, for African masks and sculptures, (many artists collected these and hung examples in their studios), prepared the way for new developments. It was logical that artists who were beginning to question the necessity of representing things 'as they look' should turn their attention to other subjects: symbols, abstract rhythms of colour and line, and the magical qualities of materials themselves. (Subjects with which primitive art had always, un-selfconsciously, been concerned.) Cubism, the movement with which the birth of modern collage is identified, did not abandon reality as a subject, but on the contrary sought to be even more real than its academic predecessors by eliminating 'tricks' of perspective and light. How to depict solid shapes on a flat picture-surface without resorting to those tricks? This was the problem that the early Cubists set themselves, and in their search they opened the door to innumerable possibilities. Showing several aspects of an object simultaneously by analysing its shape and breaking it up into a series of planes was one way of approaching the problem; putting down real materials rather than their painted imitation was another.

In Paris, in 1912, Picasso pasted a piece of printed oilcloth into his *Still-life with Chair Caning*, and wrapped a length of rope around it in lieu of a frame. During the same period, the painter Braque was introducing typeset phrases and pasted wall papers into his paintings (*The Portuguese*, 1911, and *Fruit Bowl*, 1912). A little later, Juan Gris, the Spanish painter living in Paris, used printed letters and real newspapers in his pictures.

From 1912 to 1915, Picasso and Braque (working in close association), Juan Gris, and others, made much use of collage: paper, cloth, wood, metal and sand were incorporated in their paintings and relief constructions. Collage had finally entered the heretofore sacred territory of the 'fine arts'.

Other art movements soon took up collage and adapted it to

Fig. 87 Juan Gris: *The Sunblind,* 1914. Oil and pasted papers. Courtesy of the Trustees of the Tate Gallery, London.

their own particular goals. It is impossible in such a limited space to include all the ideas, facts, and circumstances which led to the development of these movements; I have briefly summarized some of them, and the list on p. 101 gives you some suggestions for further reading.

Futurism (Cubism's chief rival from 1909 to 1914) was evolved by a group of Italian artists (Boccioni, Carra, Russolo, Severini, Balla) led by the writer Filippo Tommaso Marinetti. He had published in Paris, in 1909, the first Futurist manifesto, extolling the beauty of speed and motion and vowing to destroy museums, libraries, and academic institutions of every kind. The Futurists rebelled against the tradition that a picture is on a surface placed before the spectator (a tradition respected by the Cubists), and wanted to 'put the spectator in the centre' of the picture. These were philosophical ideas rather than painting problems; they were aiming at a 'total art' which would embrace not only painting and sculpture, but also architecture, literature, music, science, sound and light, ideas which are today being developed by artists and art schools. The academies which the Futurists rebelled against, have, in fact, largely been replaced by art 'laboratories' where such ideas can be freely explored. To depict energy, sound, continuity or memory, the Futurists used collage materials in a kaleidoscopic way, creating broken, multiple images, sometimes not unlike the reflections in a many-faceted mirror. One of the first modern 'assemblages' was Boccioni's *Fusion of a Head and Window* (1911), which includes a plaster head with pasted-on locks of real hair, and an actual window-frame.

Dada, the movement christened in 1916 at Zurich, Switzerland, by placing a finger at random on a page of a French dictionary ('dada', a child's word for a hobby-horse), was fundamentally a protest. Under a surface of wild nonsense, it expressed disillusionment with society and its contradictory values, which the war had brought into focus. What is beautiful? What is ugly? What is false? What is true? The Dada answer was that sense and nonsense, design and chance, order and chaos, belong inseparably together. This view attracted a great number of artists in Switzerland, Germany, France and New York, and Dadaist works of poetry, drama, ballet, satirical photography, painting, and collage startled the world.

Kurt Schwitters (born in Germany, 1887, died in England, 1948), deserves a special place in the history of collage. Although associated with Dada, he stands outside all movements as a poet

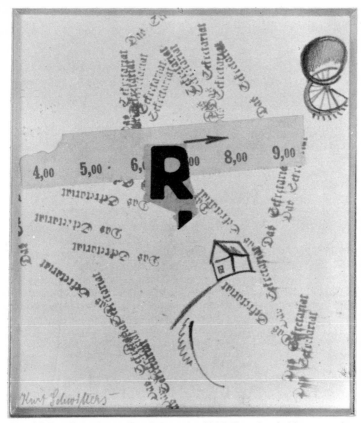

Fig. 88 Kurt Schwitters: *Das Sekretariat,* 1919. Drawing, rubber stamping, and collage. A Dada example. Courtesy Lords Gallery, London.

of the commonplace who made collage his own personal language. The usual Schwitters collages were about the size of a postcard, some even smaller, but even in these minute works, cast-off scraps acquire a radiance impossible to explain in terms of styles or techniques.

In spite of his sophistication, his works are often closer in feeling to the folk artist than to the 'professional'; his *Merzbau* (one of several begun, later destroyed in the Second World War) was a three-dimensional collage, a kind of column erected in the middle of a room, to which Schwitters, over a period of ten years, added 'found' scraps, until the structure finally pierced the three floors of his house. Schwitters had begun with traditional art training at the Dresden Academy. For a long time he painted academic portraits to earn his living; by 1919 he had begun his work in collage, which he called 'Merz' (from a fragment of print he had pasted into a picture, showing the word 'Kommerz'). He extended this name to his poetry, which he had been writing since 1917, to stories, articles, and finally to all his creative activities.

Elements of Cubism, Futurism, and other influences appear in Schwitters' collages, but they are always subordinated to a poetic, loving regard for the materials themselves, which he thoughtfully and enthusiastically collected. Our own ability to find beauty in such materials, the waste-products of our civilization, is awakened by Schwitters' candid and childlike vision.

Fig. 90 Kurt Schwitters: *Syng Ring of a Poet,* 1940. Wood, pebbles, feather, shell, rubber, etc., and oil paint. Courtesy Lords Gallery, London.

*Opposite:*
Fig. 89 Kurt Schwitters: *Mz 439,* 1922. Courtesy of the estate of Kurt Schwitters and Marlborough Fine Art Limited, London.

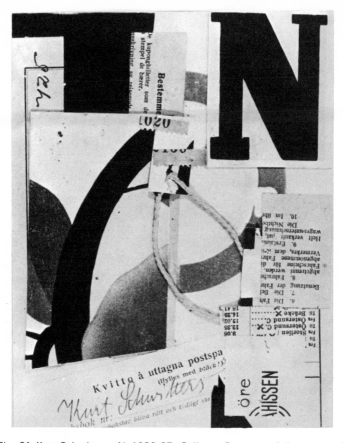

Fig. 91 Kurt Schwitters: *N*, 1936-37. Collage. Courtesy of the estate of Kurt Schwitters and Marlborough Fine Art Limited, London.

The Dada movement had produced artists who were 'anti-art': they thumbed their noses at both the artist and the public (in 1919, Marcel Duchamp had exhibited in New York a reproduction of the *Mona Lisa* which he decorated with a moustache). The technique of photomontage had particularly attracted the Dadaists, notably

Fig. 92 Kurt Schwitters: *Falling Red*, 1947. Collage. Courtesy Lords Gallery, London.

the German group: Raoul Hausmann (sometimes credited with being one of the 'inventors' of photomontage), explains, 'We called this process 'photomontage' because it embodied our refusal to play the part of the artist. We regarded ourselves as engineers and our work as construction: we 'assembled' (in French: 'monter') our work, like a fitter.' Among this group were also John Heartfield, George Grosz, and Hannah Hoech, who adopted the process and found entirely new possibilities for it.

By the early 1920's, the war was over, the Dada mood had passed, and was replaced by a new interest in science and psychology. Surrealism, the movement which took over where Dada had left off, seemed to offer a technique for exploring the unconscious; that 'new' territory which modern psychologists (such as Freud) had just begun to uncover. As defined by its founder, André Breton, Surrealism was 'pure psychic auto-matism': to speak, write, draw or paint automatically, as if in a trance, without allowing reason, aesthetic or moral preoccupa-tions to interfere. This was a process known since ancient times (the history of religion and magic is full of examples of 'automatic manifestations', variously attributed to the influence of God, gods, devils or spirits), but Surrealism was the first attempt to use this force for purposes of artistic creation. It led to the development of remarkable ideas and techniques, which have not yet been fully explored. Many artists (some of whom had been Dadaists) were drawn to this movement, among them Miro, Dali, Man Ray, Magritte, Tanguy, and Max Ernst. Of all the Surrealists, it was perhaps Ernst who made the most extensive and original use of collage, inventing an enormous number of unorthodox tech-niques to stimulate and guide his imagination (see fig. 93). A Surrealist 'classic' is Ernst's *Kindness Week or the Seven Capital Elements,* a series of collages in book form composed entirely of cut-outs from Victorian steel-engraved illustrations, which Ernst re-arranged (making a point of never touching them with pen or brush) into disturbing, often frightening, compositions.

Another artist who holds a unique place in the history of collage is Henri Matisse. During the last ten years of his life (he died in 1954), barred by illness and age from easel painting, he gave up the brush for the scissors, and paint for coloured paper. Far from being a limitation, the medium of 'papier collé' was the happy culmination of his art and his life. He had always preferred to apply colour on his canvases flat, and the use of cut and pasted coloured papers justified all his previous achievements. He himself said: 'Scissors can achieve more sensitivity than the pencil', and his magnificent cut-outs (such as the book *Jazz*) are proofs of this.

Among the other contemporary artists who have exploited the possibilities of *'papiers collès'* (literally pasted papers and generally referring to fresh, plain, coloured paper), are the English artist Ben Nicholson (in his 1939 collages) and the American A. D. F. Reinhardt; today Victor Pasmore (Great Britain), Bernard Gay (Great Britain. See fig. 33), Will Barnet (U.S.A.), Burgoyne Diller (U.S.A.), Vilmos Huszar, and others continue this tradition, making their own path within it.

Unfortunately, space does not permit the inclusion of all the names who have contributed to collage history, and likewise, I cannot hope to do justice to the ever-growing number of contemporary artists who are exploring this medium and making it their own. The works of some of them appear in this book, and I hope that you will take the trouble to discover for yourself other examples of the fascinating results of creating in collage.

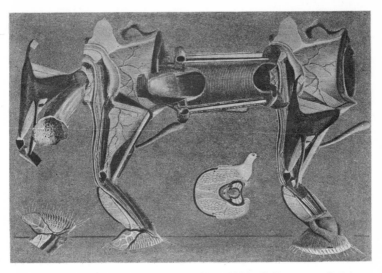

Fig. 93 Max Ernst: *The Horse, He's Sick,* 1920. Collage, pencil, ink. Collection The Museum of Modern Art, New York.

Fig. 94 Arthur G. Dove: *Grandmother,* 1925. Collage of shingles, needle-point, page from the concordance, pressed flowers. Collection The Museum of Modern Art, New York. Gift of Philip L. Goodwin.

Fig. 95 Robert Motherwell: *Cambridge Collage*, 1963. Oil and paper on board. Courtesy Marlborough-Gerson Gallery Inc., New York.

Fig. 96 Grace Hartigan: *Pure Fury*, 1965. Collage, gouache. Courtesy
Martha Jackson Gallery, New York.

Fig. 97 Lee Gatch: *October Tapestry*, 1967. Oil and collage on panel. Courtesy Staempfli Gallery, New York.

# For further reading

Collage; Personalities, Concepts, Techniques by Harriet Janis and Rudi Blesh. Pitman, London. Chilton, Philadelphia and New York.

Découpage by Dorothy Harrower. Barrows, New York.

The Art of Assemblage by William C. Seitz. The Museum of Modern Art, New York.

Dada: Art and Anti-Art by Hans Richter. Thames & Hudson, London. McGraw Hill, New York.

The Era of the Photograph by Michael F. Braive. Thames & Hudson, London.

Plastics as an Art Form by Thelma R. Newman. Pitman, London. Chilton, Philadelphia and New York.

Primitive Art by Douglas Fraser. Thames & Hudson, London.

Making Mosaics by John Berry. Studio Vista, London, 1966. Watson—Guptill, New York, 1967.

Collage and Found Art by Dona Meilach and Elvie Ten Hoor. Reinhold, New York, 1964. Studio Vista, London, 1965.

Creative Photography by Aaron Scharf. Studio Vista, London, 1965. Reinhold, New York, 1965.

*Opposite:*
Fig. 98 Jack Yates: *Mr. Elerch Evans in Bont Goch.*

# List of suppliers

Coloured papers, cardboard, etc.: F. G. Kettle, 127 High Holborn, London, W.1.

Paper, general craft supplies: Dryad Handicrafts, 22 Bloomsbury Street, London, W.C.1.

Artists' materials in general: George Rowney & Co., 10/11 Percy Street, London, W.1.

The adhesives mentioned in the book can be purchased in any hardware or stationery shop.

In U.S.A., Arthur Brown, Inc., 2 West 46 Street, New York, N.Y. 10036 or A. I. Friedman, 25 West 45 Street, New York, N.Y. 10036 are two suppliers that provide mail order service.

# Index

# Acknowledgements

The author and publishers would like to make the following acknowledgements for pictures in this book:

Figs. 1, 2, 4, 5, 7, 8 to 12, 13, 14, 15, 16, 17 to 21, 23, 24, 25, 27, 28, 29, 30, 31, 33, 34 to 37, 38, 39, 40, 41 to 44, 45, 46, 47, 53, 55, 56, 60, 61 to 65, 66, 67, 68, 69, 70, 72, 73, 74, 75, 76, 78, 79, 80, 81, 82, 83, 84, 98: photographs by Ted Sebley.

Figs. 3, 22, 49: photographs by G. N. Blake.

Figs. 6, 32: photographs by Peg Mills.

Figs. 50, 51, 52: photographs by Harry Hodgson.

Fig. 59: photograph by Jadwiga Debska.

Fig. 86: from *A Picture Postcard Album*, Thames & Hudson, London, 1961.

Fig. 88: photograph by A. C. Cooper, Ltd.

Fig. 93: photograph by Soichi Sunami.

Fig. 94: photograph by Soichi Sunami.

Fig. 96: photograph by John D. Schiff.

Fig. 97: photograph by John D. Schiff.

We would also like to thank all the artists who kindly contributed examples of their work, as well as the students and staff of the Camden Arts Centre, London, and of the Graphic Design Department at the Tottenham annex of Hornsey College of Art.